W9-BGP-284

WHALE SHARKS

▲ JULIE MURPHY

Published in the United States of America by Cherry Lake Publishing
Ann Arbor, Michigan
www.cherrylakepublishing.com

Consultants: Dominique A. Didier, PhD, Associate Professor, Department of Biology, Millersville University; Marla Conn, ReadAbility, Inc.
Editorial direction: Red Line Editorial
Book design and illustration: Sleeping Bear Press

Photo Credits: iStockphoto/Thinkstock, cover, 1, 5, 17, 20; Sleeping Bear Press, 6; Krzysztof Odziomek/Shutterstock Images, 9, 29; Dorling Kindersley RF/Thinkstock, 11; Shutterstock Images, 12; Kim Briers/Shutterstock Images, 13, 19; Paul Cowell/Shutterstock Images, 15, 16; Monika Wieland/Shutterstock Images, 23; T.W. van Urk/Shutterstock Images, 25; S. Gruene/Shutterstock Images, 27

Copyright ©2014 by Cherry Lake Publishing
All rights reserved. No part of this book may be reproduced or utilized in any form or by any means without written permission from the publisher.

Library of Congress Cataloging-in-Publication Data

Murphy, Julie.
Whale sharks / Julie Murphy.
     p. cm. — (Exploring our oceans)
  Audience: 008.
  Audience: Grades 4 to 6.
  Includes index.
  ISBN 978-1-62431-411-7 (hardcover) — ISBN 978-1-62431-487-2 (pbk.) — ISBN 978-1-62431-449-0 (pdf)
— ISBN 978-1-62431-525-1 (ebook)
  1. Whale shark—Juvenile literature. I. Title.

  QL638.95.R4M87 2014
  597.3—dc23   2013006358

Cherry Lake Publishing would like to acknowledge the work of The Partnership for 21st Century Skills. Please visit www.p21.org for more information.

Printed in the United States of America
Corporate Graphics Inc.
July 2013
CLFA11

ABOUT THE AUTHOR

Julie Murphy is an Australian children's writer. She trained in zoology and zookeeping and loves writing about animals. She also enjoys traveling and was lucky to go to Ningaloo Reef in Australia, where the whale sharks visit. Julie lives in Melbourne with her husband and daughter and their pets.

TABLE OF CONTENTS

CHAPTER 1

THE GENTLE GIANTS

Imagine swimming at the beach when you hear someone shout, "Shark!" What would you think? What would you do? Sharks are usually thought of as killers with swift bodies and sharp teeth. But that is not true for whale sharks. They are slow-moving, gentle animals. They are harmless to people.

How did whale sharks get their name? One reason is their huge size. The blue whale is the largest animal on earth. Although not as large as blue whales, whale sharks are still giants of the sea. They can grow as long as a

The whale shark is the biggest fish in the ocean.

school bus. They can weigh more than three African elephants. Whale sharks definitely deserve their title of world's largest fish. (Sharks are fish, and whales are mammals.)

Second, whale sharks have the same way of eating as many whales. They take in great gulps of water, filter out the tiny animals in it, and eat them. This is called **filter feeding**.

Whale sharks are found in the warm ocean waters near the equator. They can be found in shallow water

RANGE MAP

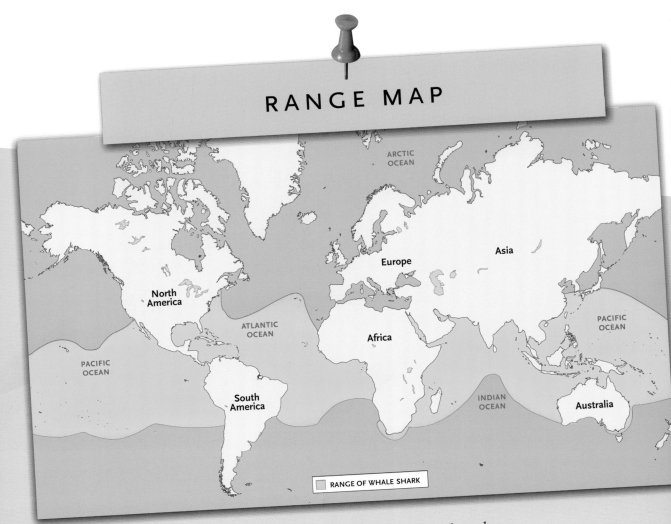

Whale sharks avoid colder waters near the poles.

close to coasts, islands, and reefs. They also swim in deep, open ocean water. Whale sharks can dive deeper than 1 mile (1.6 km) below the surface. After plunging into deep, chilly waters, they often visit sunny surface waters to warm up. Like most fish, whale sharks are **cold-blooded**. They cannot keep their bodies warm without moving to a warmer place, like shallow water.

Whale sharks swim great distances. One whale shark swam 5,000 miles (8,047 km) in 150 days. That is farther than traveling the entire length of South America. Scientists think whale sharks **migrate** along regular routes that may take years to complete. But scientists do not yet know the exact pathways. Researchers are studying whale sharks in their own regions. Then they share their results with other scientists around the world. By doing this, researchers hope to build a complete picture of where whale sharks go, what they do, and how they live. ◢

THINK ABOUT IT

READ THIS CHAPTER CLOSELY. WHAT IS ONE OF ITS MAIN IDEAS? PROVIDE TWO POINTS FROM THE TEXT THAT SUPPORT THIS.

— CHAPTER 2 —

LARGEST FISH

Imagine snorkeling near a reef when a whale shark comes into view. It would dwarf the other creatures around the reef. The whale shark is about 40 feet (12.2 m) long. It weighs around 20.6 tons (18.7 t). This is about the weight of a large school bus. Yet the giant's body is streamlined. It cuts through the water with ease. As it swims closer, its broad, flat head and stubby snout come into view. The mouth is almost as wide as the whole head. Its opening is about 5 feet (1.5 m). That is big enough for a ten-year-old kid to lie down in!

8

[21ST CENTURY SKILLS LIBRARY]

— CHAPTER 2 —

LARGEST FISH

Imagine snorkeling near a reef when a whale shark comes into view. It would dwarf the other creatures around the reef. The whale shark is about 40 feet (12.2 m) long. It weighs around 20.6 tons (18.7 t). This is about the weight of a large school bus. Yet the giant's body is streamlined. It cuts through the water with ease. As it swims closer, its broad, flat head and stubby snout come into view. The mouth is almost as wide as the whole head. Its opening is about 5 feet (1.5 m). That is big enough for a ten-year-old kid to lie down in!

Each jaw has around 300 rows of teeth. Each row has hundreds of teeth in it. You can't see them clearly because they are covered by a layer of skin. Why are whale sharks' teeth covered by skin? No one knows yet.

The whale shark has a huge mouth.

LOOK AGAIN

Look at this photograph. How is the whale shark different from what you know of other sharks?

Now the shark has come up next to you. You have a close-up view of its side. First you see the tiny eye. Next come five large gill slits. They are open wide, and inside you can see rows of **cartilage**, which hold the spongy filters in place. The shark's entire skeleton is made of cartilage. Cartilage bends more than bone. The cartilage skeleton is what makes sharks different from most other fish. Most fish have bony skeletons.

Now you see the shark's long pectoral fin. It sticks out to the side like a bird's wing and helps the shark steer. Three ridges run along the body. They end at the tall, crescent moon–shaped tail. The tail swipes from side to side and pushes the animal forward through the water.

Two dorsal fins on the whale shark's back help it swim straight without rolling over. The first fin is much larger than the second. The first fin can be more than 5 feet (1.5 m) tall.

BODY DIAGRAM

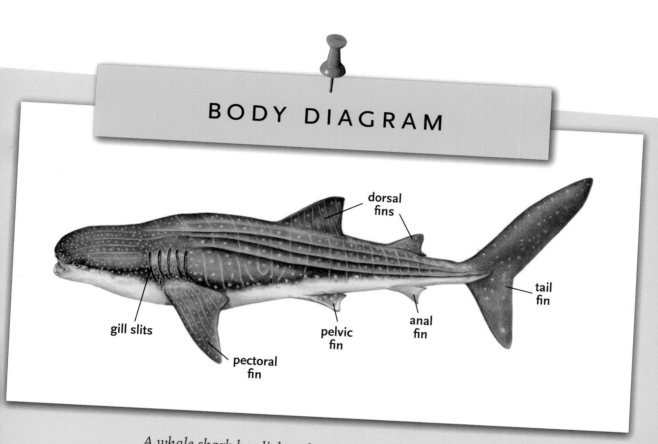

dorsal
fins

tail
fin

gill slits

anal
fin

pelvic
fin

pectoral
fin

A whale shark has light-colored spots on the top of its body.

Whale sharks swim alone or in small groups.

Whale sharks have a special color pattern called **countershading**. They are dark on top and white underneath. Countershading helps the shark hide by allowing it to blend in with its surroundings. If viewed from below, the white belly helps the shark blend in with the light surface waters above. If viewed from the top, the shark matches the deeper, darker waters underneath it. So even an animal as huge as a whale shark can hide to sneak up on prey. The shark's dark upper surface has a pattern of white spots and lines. Every whale shark has a slightly different pattern.

Each whale shark's spotted pattern is unique.

CHAPTER 3

FILTER FEEDERS

Whale sharks mostly eat tiny animals and plants called **plankton**. They also eat larger animals, such as squid, jellyfish, sardines, and tuna. Why do whale sharks have such a mixed menu? It's because of the way they eat. They filter feed.

First, they take in huge gulps of seawater. In about two hours, a whale shark can filter enough water to fill an Olympic-sized swimming pool. That is more than 650,000 gallons (2.5 million L).

Whale sharks open their mouths wide when feeding.

Once water enters the mouth it passes to the gills. The gills contain spongy filters held up by cartilage rods. When the whale shark closes its mouth, the water flows out through the gills and back into the ocean. The whale shark swallows all the food the filters catch. The filters can catch anything bigger than the width of a matchstick.

GO DEEPER

CLOSELY READ THE PREVIOUS PARAGRAPHS. WHAT IS THE MAIN IDEA? PROVIDE TWO REASONS WHY YOU THINK THIS.

A whale shark hangs in the water to feed.

Whale sharks aren't fussy about where or how they eat. They will feed near the surface or in deeper water. Sometimes they suck the water in like a vacuum cleaner. Sometimes they "hang" in the water with their heads up and mouths open, letting the water rush in. They can cruise along with their mouths open or move their heads from side to side. This sideways head movement could also be a way of sniffing out prey. There are two sensitive nostrils just above the huge mouth.

Whale sharks must eat a lot of plankton to survive. Every year they go to a few special places that have large amounts of plankton. Whale sharks time their visits to match when the plankton supply is at its peak. Ningaloo

Reef is off the west coast of Australia. This reef receives large groups of whale sharks every March and April. This is the time when the corals of the reef **spawn**. Spawning corals release large amounts of food for the whale sharks. Whale sharks usually feed alone. During the coral spawning at Ningaloo Reef, whale sharks gather and feed in groups. ◢

Whale sharks travel to Ningaloo Reef when its corals spawn.

CHAPTER 4

Pups and Adults

Scientists still have a lot to learn about the life cycle of whale sharks. Whale sharks were first identified in 1828. But before the mid-1980s people rarely saw them. Scientists do know some basic information about the life cycle of whale sharks, however.

When whale sharks **mate**, the male fertilizes the eggs inside the female's body. Male whale sharks first breed once they are about 30 feet (9.1 m) long. This is when they are between 13 and 30 years old. Scientists do not yet know when females first breed. They do not know

The whale shark's eyes are on the sides of its head.

for certain where mating occurs. Scientists have never witnessed a mating of whale sharks.

Once fertilized, the eggs start to grow inside the mother's body. The eggs hatch inside her. The babies keep growing inside the mother until they are born as live **pups**. Only one pregnant whale shark has been found. She had 300 pups. They ranged in length from 17 to 25 inches (42–63 cm).

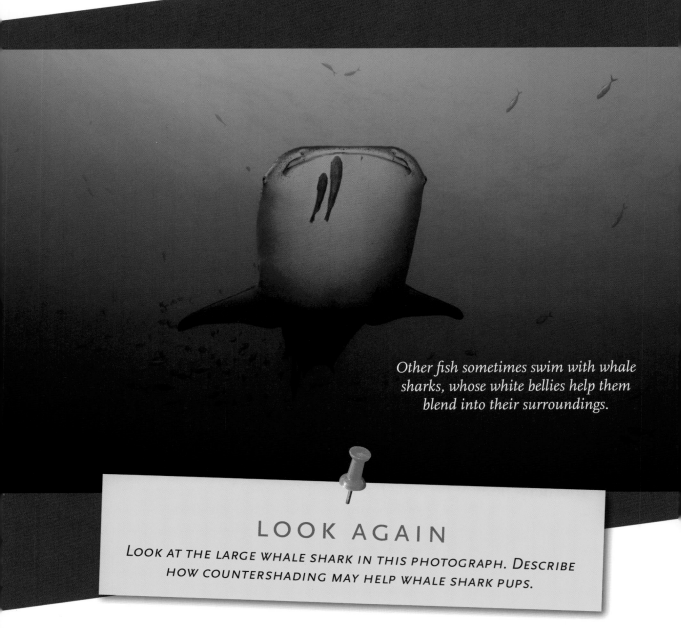

Other fish sometimes swim with whale sharks, whose white bellies help them blend into their surroundings.

LOOK AGAIN

Look at the large whale shark in this photograph. Describe how countershading may help whale shark pups.

[21ST CENTURY SKILLS LIBRARY]

Scientists still have many questions about the life cycle of whale sharks. How often do they breed? Are the pups born in special nursery areas? How many pups are born at once? How long do they live? Researchers are working hard to find answers to these questions with the help of modern technology. Spotter planes help find the animals. Soon perhaps pups will be seen. Tags on the sharks tell researchers where the sharks travel. This may help locate breeding grounds. With these tools, scientists hope to learn more about the shark's life cycle. ◢

CHAPTER 5

THREATS

What predator would take on an adult whale shark? Maybe there isn't one! Attacks on whale sharks have rarely been seen. They likely do not occur often once the sharks are full-grown. Orcas, blue sharks, and blue marlin—all smaller than the full-grown whale shark—hunt younger, smaller whale sharks.

Ocean predators are rare. However, human activities such as fishing and tourism could threaten the whale shark's future. The large, slow-swimming giants make easy targets for fishermen, especially when the sharks swim near the ocean surface. Their big dorsal fins are prized for shark fin soup. The fins fetch a high price in the markets of some Asian countries.

Orcas, or killer whales, are threats to small, young whale sharks.

If too many whale sharks are caught, the total number in the oceans will become too low. This is called **overfishing**. Some countries such as the Maldives, the Philippines, India, and Honduras have laws limiting or eliminating the hunting of whale sharks. While that's a good start, whale sharks visit the waters of around 100 different countries. Not all these countries protect whale sharks. Those countries that do are sometimes troubled by illegal fishing. Fishermen who are trying to catch other species can accidentally harm whale sharks. Sometimes boats accidentally strike the sharks too.

Many tourists jump at the chance to swim with gentle whale sharks. Tourism companies have been set up in a few places where large groups of whale sharks regularly visit to feed on plankton. While there is little risk to the tourists, some people think it might be a different matter for the sharks. The sharks are there to eat. Humans might disrupt their feeding.

Overfishing poses a threat to whale sharks.

A five-year study at Ningaloo Reef found that well-controlled tourism does not affect the whale sharks. Results showed that it is important to set and follow rules that protect the animals. Activities that could be harmful are banned. These include touching the sharks and using flash photography. Limits are set on the number of tourism companies that are allowed to operate and how close boats can get to the sharks.

Whale sharks are affected by another human-related problem: pollution. Rain can wash garbage and chemicals on the ground into drains. This pollution can eventually end up in the oceans. If swallowed by a whale shark, trash could cause injury or even death. Reducing waste and making sure to dispose of garbage and chemicals in proper ways are things people can do to prevent this risk to whale sharks.

Climate change can also threaten the whale shark's survival. Some human activity affects how fast climate change is occurring. This includes the amount of carbon

People swimming with whale sharks must follow rules in order not to harm the sharks.

LOOK AGAIN

WHAT MIGHT THE SWIMMERS IN THIS IMAGE BE THINKING? WOULD THEY FEEL THREATENED OR SAFE THAT CLOSE TO A WHALE SHARK?

dioxide and other gases that are released into the air. Climate change shifts global weather patterns and ocean temperatures. Many ocean creatures can only survive within a very specific temperature range. Sensitive ocean creatures such as corals and plankton cannot survive if the oceans become too hot or too cold. Without these, whale sharks and many other filter feeding animals would not have enough food.

The International Union for Conservation of Nature (IUCN) classifies whale sharks as Vulnerable on its Red List of Threatened Species. This means that populations could eventually become **extinct** if they are not protected. There could still be hundreds of thousands of them in our oceans. But scientists believe their numbers are decreasing. Really large whale sharks are now only rarely seen. The more researchers can learn about these fascinating creatures, the better they can understand them and protect their survival far into the future. ◣

Researchers continue to study whale
sharks in order to protect them.

THINK ABOUT IT

▲ What was the most surprising fact you learned from reading this book?

▲ Read Chapter 5 again. What is the main idea of this chapter? List three pieces of evidence that support the main idea.

▲ Find a reliable Web site about whale sharks and look around on it. Compare the information you find there with the information in this book. Is it similar or different? Why do you think it is similar or different?

LEARN MORE

FURTHER READING

MacQuitty, Miranda. *Shark*. New York: DK, 2011.

Marsico, Katie. *Sharks*. New York: Scholastic, 2011.

Musgrave, Ruth. *Everything Sharks*. Washington, DC: National Geographic, 2011.

Parker, Steve. *100 Facts on Sharks*. Thaxted, UK: Miles Kelly, 2010.

WEB SITES

Discovery Kids—Sharks
http://kids.discovery.com/gaming/shark-week

This Web site lets readers learn about shark attack survivals and play games.

National Geographic—Sharks
http://animals.nationalgeographic.com/animals/sharks

Readers discover different species of sharks, learn more about the ocean, and play games at this Web site.

GLOSSARY

cartilage (KAHR-tuh-lij) a hard, flexible tissue that forms certain parts of animals' bodies, such as a human ear or a shark's skeleton

climate change (KLYE-mit CHAYNJ) the changing of the temperature in Earth's atmosphere over a period of time, which can shift weather patterns and sea temperature

cold-blooded (KOHLD BLUHD-id) having a body temperature that changes in relation to the temperature of its surroundings

countershading (KOUN-tur-shay-ding) the light and dark coloring of an animal to help it blend into its surroundings

extinct (ik-STINGKT) no longer found alive

filter feeding (FIL-tur FEE-ding) feeding done by taking in water, filtering out animals and plants, and eating them

mate (MATE) to join together to produce babies

migrate (MYE-grate) to move from one area to another

overfishing (oh-vur-FI-shing) taking so many individuals from a place that the species' future is threatened

plankton (PLANGK-tuhn) tiny animals and plants that drift in bodies of water

pup (PUP) a baby shark

spawn (SPAWN) to produce a large number of eggs

INDEX

[21ST CENTURY SKILLS LIBRARY]